GAUDÍ

Cossetània EDICIONS

RIUDOMS

1852

Although he is born in the village of Riudoms, Antoni Gaudí spends his childhood in Reus. He does not enjoy good health, but he likes nature. He is out of doors as much as possible and tries to be in contact with trees, flowers and mountains. He will later use their shapes to construct buildings.

BARCELONA

1868

Gaudí completes his training at the
Higher School of Architecture in Barcelona.
He is just a student, but he is already showing
a very special character. After presenting his
most visionary student with his qualification,
the director of the school says: "I don't know
whether that Antoni is a madman or a
genius. Time will tell!"

MODERNISME

1878

When Gaudí begins working, the fashionable
style among architects is *Modernisme*.
They draw undulating shapes, use different
materials in the same building and imitate
classical styles, etc. It all suits Gaudí's taste
well and it is not long before he becomes
one of the most promising youngsters of the
moment.

GÜELL PALACE

1886

Before long, the industrialist Eusebi Güell provides him with his first important commission. The Güell Palace, in the centre of Barcelona, shows Gaudí's talent as a *Modernista* architect. The outstanding feature of this building, worthy of a great nobleman, is a majestic central lounge.

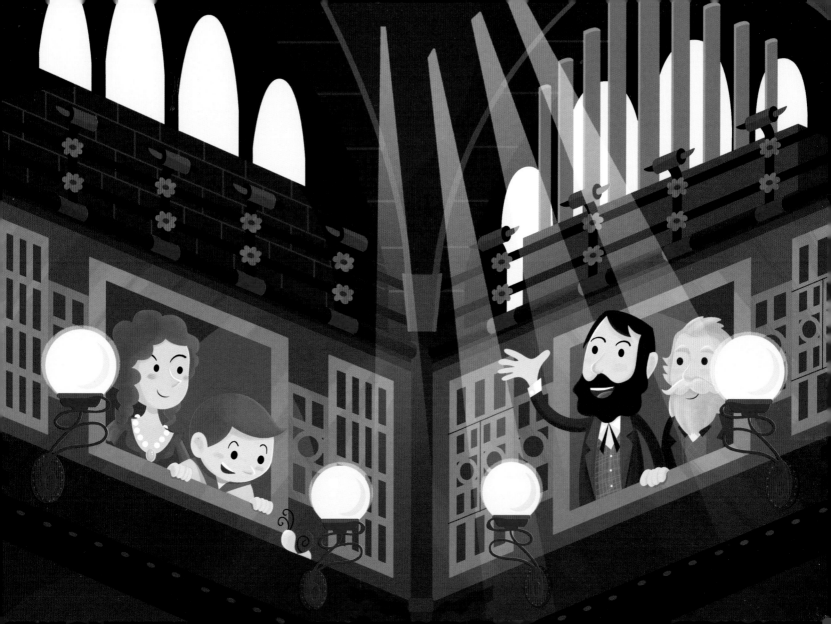

HIS OWN STYLE

◆

Pleased with Gaudí's work, Eusebi Güell entrusts other projects to the young man. Thanks to this support, Gaudí develops his own style, based on forms from nature. In his works, columns can seem like tree trunks, staircases like snail shells and towers like mountains.

THE PARK DRAGON

1900

One of Eusebi Güell's most important
commissions is the Güell Park. It was
intended to be a residential development,
but the scheme fails. Despite this, here
Gaudí leaves one of the most representative
examples of the *trencadís* mosaic technique
with ceramic fragments. The dragon
that greets visitors has become a symbol
of his work.

CASA BATLLÓ

1904

The Batlló House is one of Gaudí's most
emblematic buildings. Standing in Passeig
de Gràcia, it is the result of a commission by
Josep Batlló i Casanovas. This industrialist
only wanted to alter his house, but the
architect's imagination designed a whole
building inspired by marine forms.

MILÀ HOUSE

1906

The Milà House, also known as La Pedrera, is Gaudí's masterpiece. Commissioned by the industrialist Pere Milà i Camps, it is outstanding for its white stone and curved forms, which seem to outline a snowy mountain. On the terrace, the chimneys are shaped like knights' helms.

SAGRADA FAMÍLIA

1883-1926

Once the Milà House is finished, Gaudí
concentrates on a single work: the Sagrada
Família. In this Cathedral of the Poor,
he develops forms that no-one had ever
imagined. In the last few years of
his life, Gaudí lives in the workshop
of this building.

DEATH

Gaudí dies at the age of 75. One day, while he is walking in Gran Via, he fails to see a tram coming and it runs him over. His funeral is packed. Everyone wants to say a last goodbye to our most universal architect.

CHRONOLOGY

Antoni Gaudí
is born.

He moves
to Barcelona.

He begins the
design of the
Sagrada Família.

1852   **1863**   **1868**   **1878**   **1882**   **1886**

He begins his
studies in Reus.

He officially
qualifies as an
architect and
begins working.

Güell
Palace.

Güell
Park.

La Pedrera.

The architect
dies.

1900

1904

1906

1918

1926

Batlló House.

He devotes
himself exclusively
to the Sagrada
Família.

GAUDÍ IN BARCELONA

These are the most emblematic buildings
Antoni Gaudí constructed in Barcelona.

Avda. PEDRALBES

4 Sagrada
Família

1 Bellesguard
Tower

2 Batlló House

3 Güell Palace

5 Vicens House

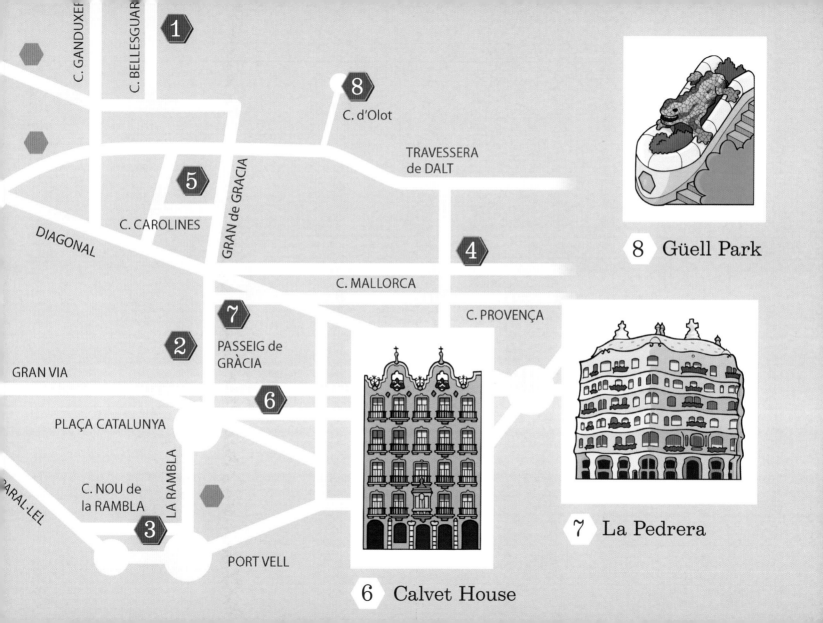

1

C. GANDUXER

C. BELLESGUAR

DIAGONAL

C. CAROLINES

5

GRAN de GRACIA

8

C. d'Olot

TRAVESSERA
de DALT

8 Güell Park

4

C. MALLORCA

C. PROVENÇA

7

PASSEIG de
GRÀCIA

2

GRAN VIA

6

PLAÇA CATALUNYA

LA RAMBLA

C. NOU de
la RAMBLA

3

ARAL·LEL

PORT VELL

7 La Pedrera

6 Calvet House

THE SEVEN DIFFERENCES

Can you find the seven differences?

WORDSEARCH

Find seven buildings by Antoni Gaudí.

Z	A	N	R	L	W	G	T	S	N	X	E	O	L	G
D	R	P	A	A	A	R	W	A	A	O	G	G	A	Ü
A	U	N	R	P	G	S	E	M	L	Y	Ü	F	P	E
Y	V	I	C	E	N	S	H	O	U	S	E	Z	E	L
A	U	A	H	D	V	E	P	E	A	M	L	A	D	L
S	Z	C	Y	R	A	V	W	G	E	T	L	W	R	P
E	F	I	T	E	P	I	N	L	E	P	C	A	E	A
W	K	O	A	R	M	S	A	I	A	M	E	S	R	L
S	A	G	R	A	D	A	F	A	M	I	L	I	A	A
X	A	Ü	M	E	S	M	I	R	Q	U	L	T	O	C
C	R	E	V	G	G	Ü	E	L	L	P	A	R	K	E
O	F	L	F	L	C	Y	S	A	B	I	R	M	N	U
N	A	B	A	T	L	L	O	H	O	U	S	E	A	Z

27

WHERE IS GAUDÍ?

Antoni Gaudí has got lost in the Sagrada Família works! Can you help find him? You will also find three palettes with glasses and four with sandwiches.

Index

The images in this book are reproduced through the courtesy of: Kyodo News/ Getty, front cover (Simone), pp. 4 (inset), 13 (bottom), 17 (bottom); Chones, front cover (U.S. flag); BUENAFOTO, front cover (gym background); Brian A Jackson, pp. 3, 22-23 (medal); picture alliance/ Getty, pp. 4-5 (main); Johnny Nunez/ Getty, pp. 6-7 (top); dpa picture alliance/ Alamy, pp. 8-9 (top); DFree, p. 9 (Simone); Cal Sport Media/ Alamy, pp. 10 (inset); Alan Edwards/ Alamy, pp. 10-11 (main); Lukas Schulze/ dpa/ AGE Fotostock, pp. 12-13 (top); A.Ricardo, p. 14 (inset); Leonard Zhukovsky, pp. 16-17 (top); John Lamparski/ Getty, pp. 18-19; Bob Levey/ Getty, p. 20 (inset); Colorado Springs Gazette/ Getty, pp. 20-21 (main).

To Learn More

AT THE LIBRARY

Adams, Julia. *101 Awesome Women Who Changed Our World*. London, U.K.: Arcturus Publishing, 2018.

Hansen, Grace. *Simone Biles*. Minneapolis, Minn.: Abdo Kids, 2017.

Sherman, Jill. *Gymnastics*. Minneapolis, Minn.: Bellwether Media, 2020.

ON THE WEB

FACTSURFER

Factsurfer.com gives you a safe, fun way to find more information.

1. Go to www.factsurfer.com.

2. Enter "Simone Biles" into the search box and click Q.

3. Select your book cover to see a list of related web sites.